2/98

ALBUQUERQUE ACADEMY
SCIENTIA AD FACIENDUM
1955

This book was donated
in honor of

Lisa Field
by

Rich Field

11-97
DATE

MISCHIEF AND DELIGHT

An Illustrated Anthology of Kittens

MISCHIEF AND DELIGHT

An Illustrated

Anthology of Kittens

CELIA HADDON

and

JESS McAREE

HEADLINE

The right of Celia Haddon to be identified as the author of the introduction to the
work has been asserted by her in accordance with the Copyright, Designs and
Patents Act 1988

First published in 1993
by HEADLINE BOOK PUBLISHING PLC
10 9 8 7 6 5 4 3 2 1

British Library Cataloguing in Publication Data
Haddon, Celia
Mischief and Delight: Illustrated Anthology of Kittens
    I. Title
636.8

ISBN 0 7472 0861 1 (Hardback)
ISBN 0 7472 4454 5 (Paperback)

Design and computer page make up by Tony and Penny Mills
Colour reproduction by Koford, Singapore
Printed and bound in Great Britain by
Butler and Tanner Limited, Frome

HEADLINE BOOK PUBLISHING PLC
Headline House
79 Great Titchfield Street
London W1P 7FN

To Wendy and to Peter
who introduced me to the joy of cats and kittens

The kitten sleeps upon the hearth,
The crickets long have ceased their mirth;
There's nothing stirring in the house
Save one, wee, hungry nibbling mouse.

DOROTHY WORDSWORTH

Author's Note

Please help homeless, neglected or ill-treated cats and kittens by
supporting cat rescue homes and charities like
the Cats Protection League and the
Feline Advisory Bureau.

CONTENTS

KITTENS IN ART AND LITERA-TURE

'K itten is in the animal world what the rosebud is in the garden; the one the most beautiful of all young creatures, the other the loveliest of all opening flowers,' wrote Robert Southey. And by doing so, he legitimised that special delight which we have in baby cats.

The charm of kittens is obvious to modern cat lovers. We would agree that these baby creatures are irresistible, and that perhaps the most memorable moments in our relationship with our cats are those innocent days of their kittenhood.

Yet, by comparing kittens with rosebuds, Southey was breaking new ground. People may have taken pleasure in kittens every since the cat found its way to Europe from ancient Egypt, but they had not thought it worth writing about. The delight they felt was a private pleasure not a public theme. While rosebuds had been in hundreds of poems throughout the long history of European literature, kittens had been ignored.

They were also rarely painted. 'Dogs outnumber cats about four to one in art, and adult cats by far outnumber kittens,' says Andrew Edney, senior vice-president of the World Small Animal Veterinary Association, who has made an exhaustive study of animals in art.

Kittens made only an occasional appearance in European art, once in the margin of a medieval manuscript and in the detail of a few seventeenth-

century paintings. This inability to see kittens as worthy of either art or literature was part of a greater blindness. Dogs were celebrated for their loyalty in poetry and prose, but puppies were barely mentioned. Childhood, itself, was little valued.

A change in attitudes started in the eighteenth century, when George Stubbs painted the kitten belonging to Miss Ann White – pictured at the start of this chapter. This is probably the first European portrait of a kitten in its own right, without its owner in the picture. At about the same time, his contemporary Thomas Gainsborough painted Miss Brummell holding a kitten.

In the same century, William Cowper, the gentle English poet, wrote *The Colubriad*, probably the first English poem devoted entirely to kittens.

It was the Romantic writers after him who opened our eyes to the charms of youth, whether of babies or of kittens. The great poet of the Lakes, William Wordsworth, took up the theme in 1804 with a poem about both. In the young he saw a spontaneous joy that is sometimes difficult for either adult humans or cats to recapture in their daily life.

Four years later Joanna Baillie published the third English poem about a kitten. At last, poets were free to celebrate these beautiful little creatures. Later still, novelists like George Eliot and Henry James were to use kittens as a benchmark for human conduct – kindness to kittens denoted a loving character. The kitten had finally taken its proper place in art and literature.

A historic moment in kitten literature came in the summer of 1782 when William Cowper devoted a whole poem to the topic of kittens. The poet had retired to the country, after a severe bout of depression, to find comfort and peace of mind in the little things of life, including kittens. This landmark poem was the result of an incident in his back yard. This is how he described it.

Passing from the greenhouse into the barn I saw three kittens looking with fixed attention at something which lay on the threshold of a door coiled up. I took but little notice of them at first but a loud hiss engaged me to attend more closely, when behold, a viper! The largest I remember to have seen, rearing itself, darting its forked tongue and ejaculating the aforementioned hiss at the nose of a kitten almost in contact with his lips. I ran into the hall for a hoe with a long handle, with which I intended to assail him, and returning in a few seconds missed him: he was gone and I feared had escaped me. Still however the kitten sat watching immovably on the same spot. I concluded therefore that, sliding between the door and the threshold, he had found his way out of the garden into the yard. I went round immediately and there found him in close conversation with the old cat, whose curiosity being excited by so novel an appearance, inclined her to pat his head repeatedly with her fore-foot; with her claws however sheathed, and not in anger, but in the way of philosophical enquiry and examination … I interposed in a moment with the hoe and performed upon him an act of decapitation.

Though Cowper's is the first English poem devoted to kittens, he admitted 'not deeming kittens worth a poet's care'. He wrote the poem in mock heroic style and called it *The Colubriad*, from the Latin word for a snake, in imitation of Virgil's epic poem, *The Aenead*.

Close by the threshold of a door nailed fast
Three kittens sat; each kitten looked aghast.
I, passing swift and inattentive by,
At the three kittens cast a careless eye;
Not much concerned to know what they did there,
Not deeming kittens worth a poet's care.
But presently a loud and furious hiss
Caused me to stop, and to exclaim – what's this?
When, lo! upon the threshold met my view,
With head erect, and eyes of fiery hue,
A viper, long as Count de Grasse's queue.

Forth from his head his forkèd tongue he throws,
Darting it full against a kitten's nose;
Who having never seen in field or house
The like, sat still and silent, as a mouse:
Only, projecting with attention due
Her whiskered face, she asked him – who are you?
On to the hall went I, with pace not slow
But swift as lightning, for a long Dutch hoe;
With which well armed I hastened to the spot,
To find the viper. But I found him not,
And, turning up the leaves and shrubs around,
Found only, that he was not to be found.
But still the kittens, sitting as before
Sat watching close the bottom of the door.
I hope – said I – the villain I would kill
Has slipt between the door and the door's sill;
And if I make dispatch, and follow hard,
No doubt but I shall find him in the yard –
For long ere now it should have been rehearsed,
'Twas in the garden that I found him first.
E'en there I found him; there the full-grown cat
His head with velvet paw did gently pat,
As curious as the kittens erst had been
To learn what this phenomenon might mean.
Filled with heroic ardour at the sight,
And fearing every moment he might bite,
And rob our household of our only cat
That was of age to combat with a rat,
With outstretched hoe I slew him at the door,
And taught him NEVER TO COME THERE NO MORE.

The Kitten and the Falling Leaves

That way look, my Infant, lo!
What a pretty baby-show!
See the kitten on the wall,
Sporting with the leaves that fall,
Withered leaves – one – two – and three –
From the lofty elder tree!…
But the kitten, how she starts,
Crouches, stretches, paws and darts!
First at one, and then its fellow,
Just as light, and just as yellow…
What intenseness of desire
In her upward eye of fire!
With a tiger-leap half-way,
Now she meets the coming prey,
Lets it go as fast, and then

Has it in her power again…
Such a light of gladness breaks,
Pretty kitten! from thy freaks, –
Spreads with such a living grace
O'er my little Dora's face;
Yes, the sight so stirs and charms
Thee, Baby, laughing in my arms,
That almost I could repine
That your transports are not mine…
Now and then I may possess
Hours of perfect gladsomeness,
– Pleased by any random toy;
By a kitten's busy joy,
Or an infant's laughing eye
Sharing in the ecstasy;
I would fare like that or this,
Find my wisdom in my bliss;
Keep the sprightly soul awake,
And have faculties to take,
Even from things by sorrow wrought,
Matter for a jocund thought,
Spite of care, and spite of grief,
To gambol with Life's falling leaf.

WILLIAM WORDSWORTH

The Kitten

Wanton droll, whose harmless play
Beguiles the rustic's closing day…
Come, show thy tricks and sportive graces,
Thus circled round with merry faces!

Backward coiled and crouching low,
With glaring eyeballs watch thy foe,
The housewife's spindle whirling round,
Or thread or straw that on the ground
Its shadow throws, by urchin sly
Held out to lure thy roving eye;
Then stealing onward, fiercely spring
Upon the tempting faithless thing.
Now, wheeling round with bootless skill,
Thy bo-peep tail provokes thee still,
As still beyond thy curving side
Its jetty tip is seen to glide:
Till from thy centre starting far,
Thou sidelong veerst with rump in air
Erected stiff, and gait awry,
Like madam in her tantrums high;
Though ne'er a madam of them all,
Whose silken kirtle sweeps the hall,
More varied trick and whim displays
To catch the admiring stranger's gaze…

The featest tumbler, stage bedight,
To thee is but a clumsy wight,
Who every limb and sinew strains

To do what costs thee little pains;
For which, I trow, the gaping crowd
Requite him oft with plaudits loud.

But, stopped the while thy wanton play,
Applauses too thy pains repay:
For then, beneath some urchin's hand
With modest pride thou tak'st thy stand,
While many a stroke of kindness glides
Along thy back and tabby sides.
Dilated swells thy glossy fur,
And loudly croons thy busy purr,
As, timing well the equal sound,
Thy clutching feet bepat the ground,
And all their harmless claws disclose
Like prickles of an early rose,
While softly from thy whiskered cheek
Thy half-closed eyes peer, mild and meek.

JOANNA BAILLIE

Fondest Greeting.

[9]

In a book about kittens, it would be wrong not to have an extract from Robert Southey's letters. For of all the Romantic writers, he was the most enthusiastic about cats. Oddly enough he only wrote one cat poem, and not a very good one at that. But all his letters show an intense love for all things feline and he wrote a longish memoir about the cats of his family. Here is his account of a kitten chasing his son, Herbert.

> We have got the prettiest kitten you ever saw – a dark tabby – and we have christened her by the heathenish name of Dido. You would be very much diverted to see her hunt Herbert all round the kitchen, playing with his little bare feet, which she just pricks at every pat, and the faster he moves back the more she paws them, at which he cries 'Naughty Dido!' and points to his feet and says, 'Hurt, hurt, naughty Dido!' Presently he feeds her with comfits, which Dido plays with awhile, but soon returns to her old game.

In Germany, the noble cause of kitten literature was taken up by Heinrich Heine, a poet and revolutionary satirist who flourished in the first half of the nineteenth century. Some of his feline poems are used to satirise human behaviour. But in a series of poems, *Songs of Creation*, he gave kittens their place in the creation story.

With best wishes for a happy Christmas

God at first the sun created,
Then each nightly constellation;
From the sweat of his own forehead
Oxen were his next creation.

Wild beasts he created later,
Lions with their paws so furious;
In the image of the lion
Made he kittens small and curious…

In matters feline, France led the world in the eighteenth century with the first prose book about cats. A century later Edmund Rostand, a poet and playwright, was one of the many French intellectuals who have loved and valued cats. This poem is called *The Little Cat*.

My small black kitten, cheeky as a page,
Plays on my table which I tolerate.
Sometimes he sits so motionless and sage
He's like a pretty living paperweight.

Nothing about him moves, not a hair of his head.
A long time he lies on my papers, black on white,
A tiny pussy with a tongue of velvet red –
Use it as pen-wiper? Well, I might…

Extremely comic when he plays,
Clumsy and kindly like a jolly bear.
Often I crouch, mimicking his ways,
When I give him a little milk down there.

Then he smells it with his delicate little nose,
Brushes the surface and with tiniest ripples,
Tastes it; then it's time to drink, he knows,
And one hears the lapping as he tipples.

He drinks, waving his tail, and without a stop,
Close to the plate his nostrils gleam –
Till the saucer's cleared of every drop,
And his rough rose tongue has left it clean.

Then licking his whiskers spick and span,
Surprised that he's finished all there was,
As if he has suddenly spotted a stain
He smoothes down his fur with a new gloss.

His blue and yellow eyes gleam like agate glows;
He half closes them, sniffs, and full length
Collapses, on his paws putting his nose,
Like a tiger stretched out in all its strength.

*L*es Chats was written by another French author, Champfleury (real name Jules Husson), in 1868 and was translated into English seventeen years later as *The Cat Past and Present*. Known then for his novels, Champfleury is probably best known now for his cat book.

A kitten is the delight of the household. Where there is one of these little creatures, a play is being performed all day long by the incomparable actor. Searchers for 'perpetual motion' need do no more than observe a kitten. Its stage is always ready. It needs but few properties; a scrap of paper, a pen, a piece of string, a pincushion, are quite enough for it to accomplish prodigies of posturing…

Even when a kitten is quiet, nothing can be more amusing. The little crouching creature with its shut eyes has such a knowing touch-me-not air. Its head hanging as though overwhelmed with sleep, its stretched-out paws, its dainty little nose, all seem to say 'Don't wake me, I am so happy.' A sleeping kitten is the image of perfect beatitude.

There are no more intrepid explorers than kittens. They make voyages of discovery into cellars and garrets, they climb on the roofs of neighbouring houses, put their little noses out of half-closed street doors, and return with a store of observation laid up for future use. Sometimes, however, this ardent curiosity leads them into dangerous places, and brings them into difficulties which they have cause to regret.

It is worthwhile to watch a kitten climbing a tree. Up it goes, from branch to branch, higher and higher, as though to enjoy the spectacle of a grand panorama. Where is it going to? It knows not. It climbs eagerly, heedless of the diminishing size of the branches, and it is only when it lays its paws upon the frail upper twigs that it begins to understand the danger of its going always straight ahead. Then it is seized with terror, and being unable to continue its course, mews in a heart-rending manner. If the tree upon which it is perched in consternation be too lofty to admit of a ladder, being brought to aid in the salvage of the poor little animal, the kitten with infinite precautions, and a heart beating almost out of its body, will let itself slide along the branches sticking its nervously convulsed claws in them…

A kitten plays a useful part in its family relations, and I advise the friends of the feline race to leave the child with its mother for at least two months, if only for the sake of the cat's health. The father and mother have reached the age of tranquillity, quietude, and even of somnolence, against which it is well to guard. The liveliness of their offspring diverts them from their idleness. The kitten will not let them sleep or dream. In the morning it jumps about its parents and licks them, thus exciting their nervous system. In vain does the father mark his irritation by the abrupt motion of his tail; the kitten pounces upon that wagging member, bites it, undeterred by any paw taps, and forces both father and mother to play with it.

In his novel, *Washington Square*, Henry James tells how a young girl's happiness is destroyed by her unloving father, Dr Sloper, and her mischief-making aunt, Mrs Penniman. At the time when Henry James wrote, kind owners always left the mother cat with one kitten (no more), rather than destroying them all. A discussion about kittens between the two adults, early on in the novel, displays Dr Sloper's lack of compassion and Mrs Penniman's irresponsibility.

Mrs Penniman exclaimed, 'I believe that last night the old gray cat had kittens?'

'At her age?' said the Doctor. 'The idea is startling – almost shocking. Be so good as to see that they are all drowned. But what else has happened?'

'Ah, the dear little kittens!' cried Mrs Penniman. 'I wouldn't have them drowned for the world!'

Her brother puffed his cigar a few moments in silence. 'Your sympathy with kittens, Lavinia,' he presently resumed, 'arises from a feline element in your own character.'

'Cats are very graceful, and very clean,' said Mrs Penniman, smiling.

In *Silas Marner*, the novelist George Eliot tells the story of a miserly weaver, whose life is changed by the arrival of a foundling baby, Eppie. The influence of a little child brings Silas Marner back to life and love. The passage starts as Eppie and he return from church. One of the signs that his life has become more loving is not just a cat on the hearth, but a cat who has been left (as cat lovers then advised) with one kitten.

Eppie put the key in the door … The sharp bark was the sign of an excited welcome that was awaiting them from a knowing brown terrier, who, after dancing at their legs in a hysterical manner, rushed with a worrying noise at a tortoiseshell kitten under the loom, and then rushed back with a sharp bark again, as much as to say, 'I have done my duty by this feeble creature, you perceive'; while the lady-mother of the kitten sat sunning her white bosom in the window, and looked round with a sleepy air of expecting caresses, though she was not going to take any trouble for them.

Silas ate his dinner more silently than usual, soon laying down his knife and fork, and watching half-abstractedly Eppie's play with Snap and the cat, by which her own dining was made rather a lengthy business. Yet it was a sight that might well arrest wandering thoughts: Eppie … laughing merrily as the kitten held on with her four claws to one shoulder, like a design for a jug-handle, while Snap on the right hand and Puss on the other put up their paws towards a morsel which she held out of the reach of both.

KITTENS IN
HISTORY

Kittens may have changed the world. We do not know what great men may have turned aside for the mew of a lost kitten, thus altering the outcome of a battle at a turning point in world events. If for want of a nail a kingdom can be lost, a kitten too may have its influence on great events.

There were great men who hated kittens – Napoleon, for one. During the second occupation of Vienna, an aide-de-camp, passing the door of the Emperor's bedroom in the Palace of Shonbrunn, heard him crying out for help. He rushed in to find Napoleon sweating with fear and lunging with his sword through a tapestry behind which was a kitten.

But men greater than Napoleon have admired the beauty of these little beings. Abu Hureira, one of the companions of the prophet Muhammed and a source for many of the Hadith (the recorded deeds and sayings of the Prophet) was known by the nickname of 'Father of the little cat', because he kept a kitten, which he carried around in his sleeve with him.

Some Western politicians have been passionate about kittens. Cardinal Richelieu, the seventeenth-century statesman, was one of these. There is also a story, perhaps put about by his enemies, that he preferred kittens to cats, and would throw his favourites out into the street when they grew up, ordering a fresh supply of little ones.

Sir Isaac Newton, when not discovering the law of gravity, is said to have invented the kitten door. His fondness for cats bemused him into an unusual lack of logic, when he had two holes made in a door, one for his cat and the other, a smaller one, for her kitten.

A love of kittens seems to have been natural to great men in America too. The philosopher Henry David Thoreau said wonderingly, 'A kitten is so flexible she is almost double; the hind parts are equivalent to another kitten with which the forepart plays. She does not discover that her tail belongs to her until you tread on it.'

Abraham Lincoln once found three kittens in the tent of General Grant. The American Civil War was raging; nevertheless Lincoln picked them up and put them under his coat. Despite all the great matters of state, he found time to make sure they had a proper home.

Mark Twain was cat mad and played billiards with one of his kittens. He used to put it into the corner pocket of the billiard table. 'Then he watches the game (and obstructs it) by the hour, and spoils many a shot by putting out his paw and changing the direction of a passing ball,' he wrote to a friend.

Finally, there are individual little cats who made their mark in history, like the kitten that climbed the Matterhorn, and others certainly had a small but important role in naval history, serving on board most of the ships and often seeing action in the great naval battles. They also serve who only sit and mew.

If kittens gave out medals to the deserving humans, Theodore Roosevelt would undoubtedly have won one. Faced with a kitten in distress, he rescued and rehomed it, as his letter from the White House to his daughter Ethel in June 1906 makes clear.

Darling Ethel,

Today as I was marching to church, with Sloane some twenty-five yards behind, I suddenly saw two terriers racing to attack a kitten which was walking down the sidewalk. I bounced forward with my umbrella, and after some active work put to flight the dogs, while Sloane captured the kitten, which was a friendly, helpless little thing, evidently too well accustomed to being taken care of to know how to shift for itself. I enquired of all the bystanders and of the people on the neighbouring porches to know if they knew who owned it; but as they all disclaimed, with many grins, any knowledge of it, I marched ahead with it in my arms for about half a block. Then I saw a very nice colored woman and a little colored girl looking out of the window of a small house with, on the door, a dressmaker's advertisement, and I turned and walked up the steps and asked if they did not want the kitten. They said they did, and the little girl welcomed it lovingly; so I felt I had gotten it a home and continued toward church.

For a cat lover, Charles Dickens wrote surprisingly little about kittens in his novels. There are the kittens kept by Mrs Corney, the hard-hearted workhouse matron in *Oliver Twist*. 'They are *so* happy, *so* frolicsome, and *so* cheerful, that they are quite companions for me,' says the matron, and one trembles for the kittens. The great novelist, however, was better to kittens in life than literature, according to his daughter Mamie who wrote this account of him.

I received a present of a white kitten – Williamina – and she and her numerous offspring had a happy home at Gad's Hill. She became a favourite with all the household, and showed particular devotion to my father. I remember on one occasion when she had presented us with a family of kittens, she selected a corner of father's study for their home. She brought them one by one from the kitchen and deposited them in her chosen corner. My father called to me to remove them, saying that he could not allow the kittens to remain in his room. I did so, but Williamina brought them back again, one by one. Again they were removed. The third time instead of putting them in the corner, she placed them all, and herself beside them, at my father's feet, and gave him such an imploring glance that he could resist no longer and they were allowed to remain. As the kittens grew older, they became more and more frolicsome, swarming up the curtains, playing about on the writing table and scampering behind the book shelves. But they were never complained of and lived happily in the study until the time came for finding them other homes.

Kittens have taken their place in a philosopher's body of work. The nineteenth-century French philosopher Hippolyte Taine adored cats. After his death twelve poems to his cats were discovered. He had hidden them from all but his closest friends. One of them is entitled *Infancy*.

The little ones are two months old and furry like a bear,
Bright-eyed as dormice, yet they snuggle catlike in their lair.
The glow of June upon them, they'll not lose their suppleness;
Within each day their frolics take up sixteen hours no less.

Standing up with arching back on velvet padded paw
They face each other; suddenly they grapple on the floor,
They roll about; but all their games express a grace so rare
That roe deer bounding through the woods are clumsy to compare.

Such gracefulness in kittens, such beauty in the roses –
Nature who is powerless over her metamorphoses,
Produces only these two perfect masterpieces rare.

Beside her, Art is tangled still in baby's swaddling clothes.
So much for human pride: what can artists then disclose?
Correggio's loves or Raphael's angels simply can't compare!

Miss Gertrude Jekyll, the famous garden designer, loved cats with a passion which meant she always had several around her. Her attitude puts to shame those mean-minded gardeners who feel that a cat is out of place in a garden. So keen was Gertrude Jekyll that she devoted a whole chapter of her book, *Home and Garden*, to cats, calling it *The Home Pussies*.

No one who has carefully and kindly brought up a kitten from its birth, could fail to find it first a charming playmate and then a firm friend. But it must be very gently and kindly treated, from the time when it makes its first excursion from its mother's basket, and long before it has any other food than its mother's milk. It must be taught to know that a hand is a kind thing. My pussies learn this for their first lesson and never forget it…

Patty is the latest importation from the outer world. She is a small cat and I fear will never be much bigger, for she had her first kittens when she was not much more than half grown. Her little boy Tommy is my latest pet, and promises to be a handsome and charming addition to our pussy-folk.

He is with me in the mornings when I open my letters, and is the one who has most appreciation of the many trade circulars brought by the early post. Most of them are printed on thin crackly paper, and when loosely crushed in the hand they make nice balls that he butts and tosses and chases all over the room. Or if I throw them into the wastepaper basket, he jumps on its edge, and tips it over and hunts out its ample contents for liberal distribution about the floor. And when we have the usual pussy-parade on the lawn at about seven on summer evenings; when, in turn with the bigger ones, he has had some good runs and jumps at the feather on the end of a whip which is the orthodox plaything, in pure delight of frisk and frolic he executes a *pas seul* on his own account, making a rapid series of monkey-jumps with high-arched back and helm hard a-port.

His mother is instructing him in the art and mystery of mousing, bringing him a mouse a day, and sitting by and watching while he goes through his mouse-drill, and finally eats up the poor little victim…

I know all my pussies in the dark not only by the feel of their coats, but by the different tone and quality of their purr. A kitten's purr is rather hard and rattly, high-pitched and unmelodious.

The story of the kitten – name unknown – that climbed the Matterhorn comes from *The Times* in 1950.

New Conquest of the Matterhorn

KITTEN'S ESCAPADE

From Our Correspondent
Geneva, September 6

A new conquest of the Matterhorn, this time by a ten-month-old black and white kitten, is reported from the Hotel Belvedere (10,820 ft), on the Hornli Ridge – the starting point for alpinists attempting to climb the mountain.

The kitten, accustomed to watch from his hotel home the dawn departure of climbers, decided one morning to follow in their footsteps. He was soon left behind, but after a long and lonely climb reached the Solway hut (12,556 ft). The next day he climbed still higher, and when night fell bivouacked in a *couloir* above the shoulder.

The next morning he was seen by a group of climbers, who passed him by, convinced that his climbing skill, if not his spirit, would be defeated by the difficult Ropes Slabs and the Root. They were wrong, and hours later the cat, miauling and tail up, reached the summit (14,780 ft), where the incredulous climbing party rewarded him with a share in their meal.

The guide, who was leading his party down the Italian side of the

Matterhorn, did not want to abandon the kitten on the top of the mountain, and as cats climb up much more easily than they climb down, the guide took him in his rucksack, brought him down to the Rifugio Principe Amedeo di Savoia (12,763 ft) and left him there until some party returning to Zermatt could take him back. He is still there, happily fattening on mice. A season of easy hunting seems a small reward for the first cat to cross the Matterhorn.

Kitten's Farewell to the Matterhorn

From Our Correspondent
Geneva, September 19

The kitten which recently conquered the Matterhorn has been brought down from the refuge hut more than 12,000 ft up on the slopes of the mountain, in which it has spent the last fortnight. With the end of the climbing season, the keeper of the hut took the kitten down to Breuil, only to find that its owner, a hotel cook, had left the place. But the kitten has found a home with an atmosphere that should be congenial to it, for it has been adopted by an Italian alpine guide.

Harrison Weir, the artist and illustrator, was a great man in feline, if not human, history. He started the first official cat show in London in 1851, with the idea of raising the status of cats, so that 'the domestic cat, sitting in front of the fire, would then possess a beauty and an attractiveness to its owner'. He also wrote *Our Cats*, from which this extract about kittens comes.

Kittenhood, the baby time especially of country cats, is with most the brightest, sprightliest, and prettiest period of their existence, and perhaps the most happy. Bright, meek-eyed, innocent, inquiring little faces, with eager eyes, peep above the basket that is yet their home. One bolder than the others springs out, when, scared at its own audacity, as quickly, and oft clumsily, scrambles back, then out – in – and out, in happy, varied, wild, frolicsome, gambolsome play, they clutch, twist, turn, and wrestle in artless mimicry of desperate quarrelling – the struggle over, in liveliest antics they chase and rechase in turn, or in fantastic mood play; 'tis but play, and such wondrous play – bright, joyous, and light; and so life glides on with them as kittens – frisky, skittish, playful kittens.

Commander William S. Donald, DSC and Bar, was a dashing naval officer in the last World War, commanding several destroyers in succession. During lulls in the warfare he was busy finding homes for kittens. He has given me this account of kittens on the ocean wave.

Georgie, a black female cat, served with me in the brand new destroyer, HMS *Ulster*, which I skippered from June 1943 to October 1944 in home waters and the Mediterranean. In March 1944 I suspected Georgie had got wed in Naples. I signalled that fact to another destroyer, adding '...the honeymoon will be spent in Capri...' But error crept in and kittens did not arrive. Georgie, who was with us at D-Day, had her kittens much later in Cardiff where we were in dock for repairs! Well, you know what Welsh cats are! One was retained aboard and others distributed to friends.

Post war, another cat, Poppet, joined me on HMS *Concord*, when I took her over as skipper in February 1947, sailing shortly after for China Station. We were alongside at Hong Kong for Christmas 1947, and one night Poppet broke ship – much to my distress. However she had also got wed, and returned on board safely before we sailed for Japanese waters. She produced four black kittens, again on my cabin bunk, in Yokohama, and again one was retained aboard and the others distributed to destroyer *Consort* and friends in Hong Kong. I always think Poppet's effort – born in Keswick, wed in Hong Kong, and produced kittens in Yokohama – was noteworthy.

KITTENS AND A MOTHER'S LOVE

Cats are extraordinarily loving to their kittens – a fact acknowledged even in the days when people believed they were evil animals. The seventeenth-century writer Edward Topsell, who warned 'it must be considered what harms and perils come unto men by this beast', declared that 'when they have littered, or as we say kittened, they rage against dogs, and will suffer none to come near their young ones'.

By the nineteenth century, the cat's maternal instincts had been elevated even further. 'Few animals exhibit more maternal tenderness, or show a greater love for their offspring,' wrote the Reverend W. Bingley in 1829. 'The assiduity with which she attends them, and the pleasure which she seems to take in all their playful tricks, afford a grateful entertainment to every observer.'

The mothering instinct is so strong that many cats are willing to accept outsiders into their family. The poet John Clare had a tame sparrow which his pet cat treated as one of her kittens. 'She woud lay mice before it as she woud for her own young … The sparrow woud often take away bits of bread from under the cat's nose & even put itself in a posture of resistance when offended as if it reckoned her no more than one of its kind.'

Modern research has confirmed that cats do, indeed, take the responsibility of motherhood very seriously. They hunt out good places for the birth, looking at several alternatives before deciding. They move the kittens from one nest site to another if they consider there is any danger.

Washing, grooming, teaching and protecting their charges is a full-time job. The most sociable of cats will all but forsake human company for the first few weeks of her kittens' life. But, if there is a cat colony, female cats will help each other – nursing one another's kittens or pooling them in communal dens.

Mother cats teach by example, often bringing live mice to the nest for their kittens to play with. We may wince at this, but it is crucial for the development of the hunting skills that humans have always valued so highly. Mother cats literally show how it is done; they also demonstrate where to defecate and how to cover up the faeces.

We can admire the school-marm in our cat, and be amazed at her tireless pursuit of excellence for her kittens. But it is her self-sacrifice for others that moves us. In her love of the weak, the helpless and the forsaken kitten, the mother cat exemplifies the altruism that we are so quick to claim uniquely for ourselves.

For cats will defend their young against terrifying odds. A cat in Yellowstone Park, USA, defended her kittens from a marauding bear with such fierceness that the bear ran up a tree in terror. The ethologist Konrad Lorenz noticed that mother cats were so fierce in defence of their young that even cat-killing dogs would retreat from their attack. Cats that were gentle in all other ways, he reported, were ready to lay down their life for their kittens.

Cats have their kittens in odd places. Any house offers a thousand equally inviting, though bizarre, alternatives. There's a nursery rhyme about a cat and a wig, which seems unlikely. Yet the eccentric naturalist Charles Waterton (who cured his sprained ankle by holding it under the Niagara Falls and who at the age of seventy-seven used to scratch the back of his head with the big toe of his right foot) actually saw a cat have her kittens in a wig, when he was a schoolboy.

Charlie's Wig

The grey cat's kittled in Charlie's wig,
The grey cat's kittled in Charlie's wig;
There's one of them living and two of them dead,
The grey cat's kittled in Charlie's wig.

From Charles Waterton's Life

One of Mr Storey's powdered wigs was of so tempting an aspect, on the shelf where it was laid up, that the cat actually kittened in it. I saw her and her little ones all together in the warm wig.

Lydia Sigourney was a nineteenth-century American writer. She started writing for children, then went on to write less successful verse for adults. She specialised in obituary poems, poetic tributes which, according to a contemporary wit, 'added a new terror to death'. *The Old Cat and Her Kittens* is one of her poems for children.

Aunt Mary's cat three snowy kittens had –
Playful, and fat, and gay; and she would sport,
And let them climb upon her back, and spread
Her paws to fondle them; and when she saw
Her mistress come that way, would proudly show
Her darlings, purring with intense delight.

But one was missing; and Grimalkin ran
Distracted, searching with a mother's haste,
Parlour, and garret, sofa, box, and bed,
Calling her baby with a mournful cry.
And questioning each creature that she met,
In her cat language, eloquently shrill.
And then she left the house. Two hours passed by,
When dragging her lost treasure by the neck,
She joyous laid it with its sister train,
Who mewed their welcome, and with raptured zeal
Washed and rewashed its velvet face and paws.

It had been trusted to a lady's care,
By my aunt Mary, out of pure good will
To Pussy, fearing she might be fatigued
By too much care and nursing. But she sought
From house to house, among the neighbours all,
Until she found it, and restored again
To her heart's jewels.

                    One full month she fed
And nurtured it. Then in her mouth she took
The same young kitten, and conveyed it back
To the same house, and laid it in the lap
Of the same good old lady, as she sat
Knitting upon the sofa. Much surprised,
She raised her spectacles to view the cat,
Who with a most insinuating tone,
Fawning and rubbing round her slippered foot,
Bespoke her favouring notice.

                    This is true –
Aunt Mary told me so. Did Pussy think
Her child too young for service? And when grown
To greater vigour, did she mean to show
Full approbation of her mistress' choice,
By passing many a nearer house to find
The lady that its first indentures held?

Victorian England saw a positive flood of literature about pets. William Gordon Stables was an eccentric writer who toured Britain in a two-horse caravan with his coachman, valet, dog, and African grey parrot which he used to serenade with a guitar. He wore full Highland dress and advised cold baths and hot porridge for boys with 'problems'. He was, however, sound on cats, as his book, *Cats: Their Points and Characteristics with Curiosities of Cat Life*, makes clear.

> Cats of the right sort never fail to bring up their kittens in the way they should go and soon succeed in teaching them all they know themselves. They will bring in living mice for them, and always take more pride in the best warrior-kitten than in the others. They will also inculcate the doctrine of cleanliness in their kits, so that the carpet shall never be wet. I have often been amused at seeing my own cat bringing kitten after kitten to the sand-box, and showing them how to use it, in action explaining to them what it was there for. When a little older she entices them to the garden … You always find that honest cats have honest kittens…

Cats will go through fire and water to save the life of their kittens and fight to the bitter end to protect them … Cats have been known to leap gallantly into the water after a drowning kitten and bring it safely to land. A case occurred only a few days ago. Some lads stole a cat's only kitten, and after playing with it all day, proposed drowning it. With this intention they went to a mill-dam, and threw it far into the water. But the loving mother had been waiting and watching not far off, and, stimulated by the drowning cry of her kitten, she bravely swam towards it and brought it to shore. I know another instance of a cat that saved the life of kittens that belonged to another cat. Her own kittens had been drowned a whole week before, but evidently she had not forgotten the loss; and one day, seeing four kittens being drowned in a pool, she plunged in and seized the largest, brought it to the bank, and marched off with it in triumph. She reared it carefully. The children baptised it Moses, very appropriately too; and it is now a fine large Tom-tabby.

Kittens, like children, learn the lessons of adulthood through play. But they also sometimes need discipline from their mothers. Here Leigh Hunt, the poet and essayist, describes one of these episodes:

We remember being much amused with seeing a kitten manifestly making a series of experiments upon the patience of its mother – trying how far the latter would put up with positive bites and thumps. The kitten ran at her every moment, gave her a knock or a bite of the tail; and then ran back again, to recommence the assault. The mother sat looking at her, as if betwixt tolerance and admiration, to see how far the spirit of the family was inherited or improved by her sprightly offspring. At length, however, the 'little Pickle' presumed too far, and the mother, lifting up her paw, and meeting her at the very nick of the moment, gave her one of the most unsophisticated boxes of the ear we ever beheld. It sent her rolling half over the room, and made her come to a most ludicrous pause, with the oddest little look of premature and wincing meditation.

A nineteenth-century book, the Reverend W.B. Daniel's *Supplement to the Rural Sports*, published in 1813, tells the story of a cat who took two kittens back to her own home. Is this another example of a cat's remarkable homing abilities? Or is it a case of mistaken identity?

In 1810, this cat was carried, by a lady, from Edinburgh to Glasgow in a basket, in a close carriage, and was carefully watched for two months. At the end of that period, she produced two kittens, and was then left to her own discretion, which she employed by disappearing with her kittens. The Glasgow lady wrote to her friend at Edinburgh, deploring her loss, and Puss was supposed to have sought some new abode, until about a fortnight after her non-appearance at Glasgow, her well-known mew was heard at the door of her former mistress, in Edinburgh. There she was discovered with her young offspring, they in the best condition, she very thin and poor.

It is clear she could only have carried one kitten at a time. The distance from Edinburgh to Glasgow is forty miles, so in returning, she must have travelled one hundred and twenty, and her prudence must have suggested the mode of travelling in the night, with many other circumstances, for the safety of her kittens. Her beauty was the original cause, for the request, of her removal. When she was admitted at the door of her old habitation, she brought one kitten up in her mouth, and deposited it in the corner of the drawing room, which she always occupied, then returned for the second, and afterwards seated herself very composedly, without taking particular notice of any of the company present.

From The Last Dying Speech and Confession of Poor Puss

But kicking, and beating, and starving, and that
I have borne with the spirit becoming a cat:
There was but one thing which I could not sustain,
So great was my sorrow, so hopeless my pain.

One morning, laid safe in a warm little bed,
That down in the stable I'd carefully spread,
Three sweet little kittens as ever you saw,
I hid, as I thought, in some trusses of straw.

I was never so happy, I think, nor so proud,
I mewed to my kittens, and purred out aloud,
And thought with delight of the merry carousing
We'd have, when I first took them with me a-mousing.

But how shall I tell you the sorrowful ditty?
I'm sure it would melt even Growler to pity;
For the very next morning my darlings I found
Lying dead by the horse-pond, all mangled and drowned.

Poor darlings, I dragged them along to the stable
And did all to warm them a mother was able;
But, alas all my licking and mewing were vain,
And I thought I should never be happy again.

ANN TAYLOR

A cat's mother love extends further than the embrace of her own kittens. The eighteenth-century clergyman and naturalist Gilbert White reported on a cat's tendency to adopt other animals in his *Natural History of Selbourne.*

My friend had a little helpless leveret brought to him, which the servants fed with milk in a spoon, and about the same time his cat kittened and the young were despatched and buried. The hare was soon lost, and supposed to be gone the way of most foundlings, to be killed by some dog or cat. However, in about a fortnight, as the master was sitting in his garden in the dusk of the evening, he observed his cat, with tail erect, trotting towards him, and calling with little short inward notes of complacency, such as they use towards their kittens, and something gambolling after, which proved to be the leveret that the cat had supported with her milk, and continued to support with great affection…

This strange affection probably was occasioned by that desiderium, those tender maternal feelings, which the loss of her kittens had awakened in her breast.

Andrew Lang, best known for his fairy books for children, tells the story of a cat trying to provide for her kittens. It is not an impossible story. Cats living in a community, where there is enough food, do take in and nurse each other's kittens.

> An old lady cat felt that she was dying, before her kittens were weaned. She could hardly walk, but she disappeared one morning, carrying a kitten, and came back without it. Next day, quite exhausted, she did this with her other two kittens, and then died. She had carried each kitten to a separate cat, each of which was nourishing a family, and accepted the new fosterling. Can anything be wiser or more touching? This poor old cat had memory, reflection, reason. Though wordless, she was as much a thinking creature as any man who makes his last will and testament.

Wishing you an A (mews) ing Christmas.

Cats seem blind to danger where the lives of their kittens are concerned. If necessary, they don't hesitate to make the ultimate sacrifice. Philip M. Rule, in his book *The Cat*, tells this moving story, from the night of a terrible fire at Lusby's Music Hall, London, on 20 January 1884:

Mr Crowder, one of the proprietors of the hall, possessed a favourite tabby and tortoiseshell cat, which was well known to the frequenters of the hall. The cat had a family of four kittens, which she was allowed to keep in a basket at the rear of the stage. Soon after the fire was discovered, the cat was seen rushing about frantically. She several times attempted to make her way down the corridor in the direction of the stage, but each time was beaten back by the smoke. Presently she reappeared with one of the kittens in her mouth. This she laid carefully down at her master's feet in the small hall which the fire had not touched. Again she rushed through the smoke, and again reappeared with a kitten, and this manoeuvre she repeated the third time.

She was now apparently half-blinded and choked by the smoke she had passed through, and it was thought she would be content; but she seemed unable to rest while she knew that one of her kittens was still in danger; and giving a look at the little struggling group on the floor, the cat, evading someone who tried to stop her, once more dashed down the corridor towards the seething mass of flames, which by this time had enveloped the stage and the lower end of the hall. Her return was anxiously awaited, but she did not come back.

Afterwards, when examining the ruins, some of the firemen came across the charred and blackened remains of the mother and kitten, lying side by side where the fire had overtaken them.

KITTENS, MORE KITTENS, AND STILL MORE KITTENS

For those whose beloved cat is expecting kittens, there have been days of anticipation. Nothing could be more delicious than the sight of the favourite cat purring over, say, three tiny bundles of teeming fur.

But as the feline mother's tummy swells, human confidence falters. The devoted owner eyes the cat's every move, minutely examining the quantity of food she is eating, the exercise she takes, whether she has grown since yesterday. Daily revising upwards, you feel panic setting in. How many kittens will she have? Five ... six ... more? Then what?

This is the Great Kitten Dilemma. As the Victorian novelist, Lord Lytton, put it: 'Nature rarely inflicts barrenness on the feline tribe; they are essentially made for love, and love's soft cares; and a cat's lineage outlives the lineage of kaisars!'

Put another way, female cats are capable of producing 200 kittens in their lifetime. If you start with a single pair of breeding cats, in five years' time (if all the kittens survive) there will be as many as 65,536 kittens and cats. Before the advent of spaying female cats in the 1940s, there was no way to stop this prodigious fertility.

No wonder therefore that kittens turn up, often quite unexpectedly, at the back door of houses, outside large office blocks, in the dustbin area of hospitals, or even at motorway service stations. Some of these little waifs

find a rescuer. Men and women who never intended to have a cat find themselves helpless to resist the kitten's appeal.

Kittens also appear, as if by magic, in even odder places. One was discovered by a young officer, Orde Browne, in the Crimean trenches – lost and forlorn in a dead Russian soldier's knapsack. The officer named him Russking, and he then spent a full and happy life in the kitchen of the Brownes' country house, much admired by the children of the family for his romantic past. Alexandre Dumas's cat, Mysouff II, turned up in the cellar of his house. Horace Walpole's cat, Harold, 'was found on the Goodwin Sands'.

Other kittens, purchased for their prestigious pedigree, arrive more conventionally in a new cat box. But however acquired, kittens immediately present their new owners with the difficulty of naming them. Some do this on the spur of the moment. In the eighteenth century the Countess of Strathmore surprised guests by leaving a dinner party saying she was going to 'the christening of some kittens'.

Others give thought to the name. 'Names are serious things,' wrote Robert Southey, 'and much ingenuity has been exerted in inventing appropriate ones, not only for man and beast, but for inanimate things.' Southey, himself, gave his cats highbrow names like Virgil, Dido, Ovid, Prester John, and Rumpelstilzchen.

To do full justice to the cat and yet to find a name easy enough for use every day is difficult. 'They say the test of [literary power] is whether a man can write an inscription,' wrote Samuel Butler in his Notebooks. 'I say "Can he name a kitten?" And by this test I am condemned, for I cannot.'

Most cat owners, when presented with endless litters of kittens, face the luckless task of persuading friends to take them on. In *The Immortal Cat*, the Czech dramatist Karel Čapek outlines the difficulty.

I always used to be of the opinion, may the deuce take them, that I had heaps of acquaintances, but from the time that Pudlenka threw herself into producing kittens, I found that in this life of ours I was terribly alone; for instance, I had no one to present with the twenty-sixth kitten. When I had to make myself known to someone I mumbled my name, and said: 'Don't you want a kitten?' 'What kitten?' they inquired dubiously. 'I don't know yet,' was my general answer; 'but I think that I shall be having some kittens again.' Soon I began to have the feeling that people were avoiding me; perhaps it was out of envy because I had such luck with kittens. According to Brehm, cats bear young twice a year; Pudlenka had them three to four times a year without any regard to the seasons. She was a supernatural cat.

There is even a poem about the Great Kitten Dilemma, written by the nineteenth-century German poet and novelist Theodor Woldsen Storm and entitled *About Cats*.

Last May day my cat gave birth
To six enchanting little kittens,
May kittens, all white with little black tails.
It certainly was a delightful nursery basket!
The cook, however – for cooks are cruel,
And human kindness never flourishes in a kitchen –
Wanted to drown five of the six.
Five white, black-tailed kittens
This wicked woman wanted to murder.
I soon saw to her! May heaven bless
My human kindness! The dear little kittens,
They grew up, and soon they were parading,
Tails in air, throughout the house and yard.
And in spite of the cook's fiercest looks
They grew and practised their little voices
Outside her window at night.
And I, watching them grow like that,
I praised myself and my humanity…

One year has passed, and the kittens now are cats,
And it is May Day! How shall I describe
The spectacle before me!
Throughout the house, from cellar to attic,
In every corner there is a nursery!
Here is one, and there another little cat,
In cupboards, baskets, under tables, under stairs,
Even the old one – I dare hardly say it! –
Is in the cook's virginal bed.
And each, yes, each of the seven cats
Has seven – would you believe it! – seven little kittens,
May kittens, all white with black tails!
The cook is furious, I fail to dampen
The blind rage of this woman;
She wants to drown all forty-nine!
And I – oh dear, my head is spinning –
Oh, human kindness, how will I safeguard you!
What shall I do with fifty-six cats!

Here is the same dilemma, this time described more positively by the poet Stevie Smith. Office workers can usually disperse surplus kittens amongst their workmates. Indeed, many a firm's staff members all play host to kittens from the same corporate cat.

Our Office Cat

Our Office cat is a happy cat
She has had two hundred kittens
And every one has been adopted into happy homes
By our cat-loving Britons.

In many cases it is a kitten that chooses its new owner. That is how Mysouff II acquired Alexandre Dumas, the French novelist. Mysouff was 'an Antony', meaning a foundling under the protection of St Antony, who finds lost things for those who invoke his aid.

There is always a pleasure in coming home again after an absence. I was glad to come back, and looked about me with a pleased smile. As I glanced from one familiar object to another, I saw, upon a seat by the fire, a thing like a black and white muff, which I had never seen before. When I came closer, I saw that the muff was a little cat, curled up, half asleep, and purring loudly. I called the cook, whose name was Madame Lamarque.

'What I do not know is, where this new guest of mine comes from.' And I pointed to the cat.

'Ah, sir!' said Madame Lamarque in a sentimental tone, 'that is an antony.'

'An antony, Madame Lamarque! What is that?'

'In other words, an orphan – a foundling, sir.'

'Poor little beast!'

'I felt sure that would interest you, sir.'

'And where did you find it, Madame Lamarque?'

'In the cellar – I heard a little cry – miaow, miaow, miaow! and I said to myself, "That *must* be a cat!" … I went down myself, sir, and found the poor little thing behind the sticks. Then I recollected how you had once said, "We ought to have a cat in the house."'

'Did I say so? I think you are making a mistake, Madame Lamarque.'

'Indeed, sir, you did say so. Then I said to myself, "Providence has sent us the cat which my master wishes for."'

[51]

Kinder men than Dumas (who later put Mysouff on trial for eating his birds) go out looking for kittens in need. Samuel Butler, the novelist, describes in his notebooks how he rescued a kitten.

I must have a cat whom I find homeless, wandering about the court, and to whom, therefore, I am under no obligation. There is a Clifford's Inn euphemism about cats which the laundresses use quite gravely: they say people come to this place 'to lose their cats'. They mean that when they have a cat they don't want to kill, and don't know how to get rid of, they bring it here, drop it inside the railings of our grass-plot, and go away under the impression that they have been 'losing' their cat. This happens very frequently and I have already selected a dirty little drunken wretch of a kitten to be successor to my poor old cat. I don't suppose it drinks anything stronger than milk and water but so much milk and water must be bad for a kitten that age – at any rate it looks as if it drank; but it gives me the impression of being affectionate, intelligent and fond of mice, and I believe, if it had a home, it would become more respectable; at any rate, I will see how it works.

Some kittens are too wild to be rescued. Andrew Lang, famous two generations ago for his books for children, was a cat lover. In *The Animal Story Book* which was published in 1896, he wrote about kittens he noticed in a London railway station.

Trains seem to have a special fascination for cats, and they are often to be seen about stations. For a long while one was regularly to be seen travelling on the Metropolitan line, between St James's Park and Charing Cross, and a whole family of half-wild kittens are at this moment making a playground of the lines and platforms at Paddington. One will curl up quite comfortable on the line right under the wheel of a carriage that is just going to start, and on being disturbed bolts away and hides itself in some recess underneath the platform. Occasionally you see one with part of its tail cut off, but as a rule they take wonderfully good care of themselves. The porters are very kind to them, and they somehow contrive to get along, for they all look fat and well-looking, and quite happy in their strange quarters.

Most cat books are written by cat breeders who hope people will buy a kitten, rather than acquire a free one. Philip M. Rule, who wrote *The Cat* as long ago as 1887, assumed that the arrival of a kitten would be the arrival of a wanted pet.

To begin towards the beginning, we may suppose that a charming little kitten, of about ten or twelve weeks, has been deposited in its new home. Being an innocent, simple, happy-tempered little creature, it will make itself at home in so pleasing a manner as to gain the approval, if not the affection, of every kind-hearted person in the house. No animal is instinctively cleaner in its habits, in every way, than is the cat. Week by week the kitten increases in strength and vivacity. Do not discourage or check the young cat in its sportiveness, although it may be a little too rough in its vivacious evolutions. The most skittish kittens usually make the best cats. The cat is an animal of naturally a very strong will, being most impatient of control, and the kitten that is allowed quietly to enjoy unmolested freedom of purpose in its queer little ways and freaks will develop, under good treatment, into a noble-spirited and well-behaved cat.

Choosing Their Names

Our old cat has kittens three –
What do you think their names should be?

One is tabby with emerald eyes,
  And a tail that's long and slender,
And into a temper she quickly flies
  If you ever by chance offend her.
    I think we shall call her this –
    I think we shall call her that –
Now, don't you think that Pepperpot
  Is a nice name for a cat?

One is black with a frill of white,
  And her feet are all white fur,
If you stroke her she carries her tail upright
  And quickly begins to purr.
    I think we shall call her this –
    I think we shall call her that –
Now, don't you think that Sootikin
  Is a nice name for a cat?

One is tortoiseshell, yellow and black,
  With plenty of white about him;
If you tease him, at once he sets up his back,
  He's a quarrelsome one, ne'er doubt him.
    I think we shall call him this –
    I think we shall call him that –
Now, don't you think that Scratchaway
  Is a nice name for a cat?

THOMAS HOOD

[55]

KITTENS AND
CHILDREN

Children and kittens go together in nursery literature. It is not just because both are young and playful: puppies, which are just as delightful, are not regarded as good playmates for babies. For puppies are slobbery and much of the time incontinent, which makes adults disapprove of them. Kittens, on the other hand, have bladder and bowel control well beyond that of human young. It is this, I think, that accounts for their popularity with mothers, and thus in nursery literature. This link between kittens and children has its counterpart among children themselves. Children identify with animals, knowing that animals would talk back, if they could. For with the wisdom of the simple-minded, children understand that there is communication, though non-verbal, between humans and felines.

It is probably easier for children to identify with kittens, with their non-stop playing, than with sleepy adult cats. Besides, kittens are so vulnerable and children are too, sometimes finding adults frightening and occasionally downright unkind. Both young things share a helplessness in the face of cruelty.

When the nineteenth-century children's writer Mary Howitt composed a poem about the escape of a kitten, the children reading it could have identified with the kitten's adventure, just as later children have identified with

[57]

Orlando the Marmalade Cat's three kittens, Tinkle, Pansy and Blanche.

Another reason for the popularity of kittens in the nursery is their lack of fear. While adult cats usually move away from a demanding toddler, kittens will stay to be picked up and played with. No wonder children like playing with kittens. Dressing up kittens, for instance, is fun for children, though not at all fun for the poor little animals squirming in doll's garments.

According to a Victorian book on cats, kittens 'are generally the delight of young children, and make charming playmates when treated gently, and not simply made toys of'. Gertrude Jekyll, the gardening writer, understood this and put on a special pussies' tea party for a visiting child – a tea party also enjoyed by the kittens and cats.

Some kittens in nursery literature are there for the purpose of painting a moral lesson for children. 'Be sensible as the little kitten,' wrote one severe Victorian writer after telling the story of a kitten who nursed baby chickens. 'Don't stand on your dignity, or keep upon the roof, in a fit of the sulks: but jump down, and shake such feeling off with a game of good-natured play.'

Kittens also romp through nonsense literature. Writers like Mark Twain and Christina Rossetti have contributed to the kitten nonsense canon. According to her brother (who inherited a kitten from her), Christina Rossetti had a half-Persian cat called Muff, and in her rhymes for children, kittens as well as cats make an appearance.

Indeed such rhymes favour kittens above puppies, despite the difficulty of rhyming kitten with anything other than mitten. So it seems suitable that it was a kitten who was responsible for the greatest nonsense story of all, Alice's adventures through the looking glass.

W.H. Davies, who was living as a tramp when his poems were first published in 1907, wrote several poems about cats. In a series of alphabet poems, a black kitten appears in the one about H.

H is for Hedge

I climb a tree to bring them down –
The yellow eyes of my black kitten;
The laurel hedge that's left behind –
Whose shoulders measure three feet wide –
Is swaying lightly in the wind.

But when I looked from my high place,
With my black kitten safely tucked
From danger, under my left arm –
I saw that laurel's thick, broad back
Was wriggling like the thinnest worm.

The Dunce of a Kitten

Come, Pussy, will you learn to read?
I've got this pretty book:
Nay, turn this way, you must indeed:
Fie, there's a sulky look.

Here is a pretty picture, see,
An Apple, and great A:
How stupid you will always be,
If you do nought but play.

Come, A, B, C, an easy task,
What anyone could do:
I will do anything you ask,
For dearly I love you.

Now how I'm vexed you are so dull,
You have not learnt it half:
You'll grow a downright simpleton
And make the people laugh.

Mamma told me so, I declare,
And made me quite ashamed;
So I resolved no pains to spare,
Nor like a dunce be blamed.

Well, get along, you naughty kit,
And after mice go look!
I'm glad that I have got more wit –
I love my pretty book.

ANN AND JANE TAYLOR

Victorians used animal stories to give children lessons in moral behaviour. *Stories of the Sagacity of Animals*, published in 1888, was the tale of a dead kitten with a neat if unconvincing moral at the end.

> Dr Good had a cat which used to sit at his elbow hour after hour while he was writing, watching his hand moving over the paper. At length Pussy had a kitten to take care of, when she became less constant in her attendance on her master. One morning, however, she entered the room, and leaping on the table, began to rub her furry side against his hand and pen, to attract his attention. He, supposing that she wished to be let out, opened the door; but instead of running forward, she turned round and looked earnestly at him, as though she had something to communicate. Being very busy he shut the door upon her, and resumed his writing. In less than an hour, the door having been opened again, he felt her rubbing against his feet; when, on looking down, he saw that she had placed close to them the dead body of her kitten, which had been accidentally killed and which she had brought evidently that her kind master might mourn with her at her loss…
>
> Observe how, in her sorrow, Pussy went to her best friend for sympathy. Your best earthly friends are your parents. Do not hesitate to tell them your griefs; and you will realise that it is their joy and comfort to sympathise with you in all your troubles, little or great, and to try to relieve them.

Mother Tabbyskins

Sitting at the window,
In her cloak and hat,
I saw Mother Tabbyskins
The *real* old cat.

    Very old, very old,
    Crumpletey and lame;
    Teaching kittens how to scold –
    Is it not a shame?

Kittens in the garden,
Looking in her face,
Learning how to spit and swear –
Oh, what a disgrace!

    Very wrong, very wrong,
    Very wrong and bad;
    Such a subject for our song
    Makes us all too sad.

ANONYMOUS

In *Tales in Verse for Young People* by Mary Howitt we find this poem, *The Kitten's Mishap*. Mary Howitt, a Quaker, was one of the humanitarian women who tried to persuade children to be kind to animals.

Now, the tale that I had in my mind to rehearse
Was related by Will, though not told in verse:
Said Willy, 'The cat had a kitten that lay
Behind my bed's head, on a cushion of hay;
A beautiful kit, though a mischievous elf,
And given to prowling about by itself.
Now it happened, one day, as I came from my work,
Before I had put by my rake and my fork,
The old cat came up, and she pawed and she mewed,
With the woefulest visage that ever I viewed,
And she shewed me the door and she ran in and out;
I couldn't conceive what the cat was about!

At length, I bethought that the creature was good,
And she should have her way, let it be what it would;
And no sooner she saw me inclined to obey,
Than she set up her tail, and she scampered away
To a pond not far off, where the kitten I found
In a bottomless basket, just sinking, half drowned.
However it got there I never could tell,
For a cat hates the water – but so it befell.
Perhaps some bad boy this action had done,
To torture the kitten and then call it fun;
Yet that I don't know; but I soon got her out,
And a terrible fright she had had, there's no doubt.
'Twas a pitiful object, it drooped down its head,
And Peggy for some time declared it was dead.
But its heart was alive, spite the panic and pain,

And it opened its eyes and looked up again;
And we gave it some milk, and we dried its wet fur,
And oh what a pleasure there was in its purr!
At length when we saw that all danger was over,
And that well warmed and dried, it began to recover,
We laid it in bed, on its cushion of hay,
And wrapped it up snugly and bade it 'good-day'.
And then its poor mother gave over her mourning
And lay down and purred like a wheel that was turning;
And she and the kitten by care unperplexed,
Slept, purred, and scarce stirred all that day and the next;
Then scarcely a trace of her trouble she bore,
Though meeker and graver than ever before.'
So here ends my tale of this watery disaster,
Of the cat and the kitten and their little master.

When Gertrude Jekyll planned a pussies' tea party for her nine-year-old niece, she ordered up fresh herrings which 'were boiled and held in readiness'. Her niece then sent out invitation cards.

Next day, early in the afternoon, we prepared the feast. The invited guests were four grown pussies and two kittens so we got ready four large and two small saucers. First a thick strip of fish was laid right across each saucer; an equal strip of cold rice pudding met it transversely, forming a cross-shaped figure that left four spaces in the angles. Thick cream was poured into these spaces and the solid portion was decorated with tiny balls of butter, one rather larger in the middle, and two smaller on each of the rays. A reserve of fish and cream was to be at hand to replenish the portions most quickly exhausted.

In the middle of the sitting room we placed a small, rather low, round table; and four stools were ranged round for the bigger pussies. As the hour for the feast drew near, much was the wondering as to how the guest would behave. They were to sit on the stools with their fore-paws on the edge of the tablecloth. We decided not to have flowers because it would have overcrowded the space, as the two kittens were to be allowed to sit on the table.

At last the hour came, and meanwhile the excitement had grown intense. Five grown-ups were present, all as keenly interested as the little girl. The pussies were brought and placed on their stools, and the kittens, Chloe and Brindle, were put up to their saucers upon the table. To our great delight they all took in the situation at once; there was only a little hesitation on Maggie's part; she thought it was not manners to put her paws on the tablecloth; but this was soon over-come, and they all set to work as if they were quite accustomed to tea parties and knew that nice behaviour was expected.

It was good to watch the pleasure of my little niece. She stood per-fectly silent and still, with hands half raised, mouth a little open, and big eager eyes drinking in the scene, as if she thought it would van-ish if she made a movement. Meanwhile the small guests were steadily eating away at their portions. Pinkieboy, as became the old-est and heaviest, finished his first, and after licking his saucer quite clean, and then his own lips, he looked round and clearly said, 'That was very good, and please I should like a little more, especially fish and cream.'

When they had all done there was a grand purring and washing of paws and faces before they got off their stools, and as they dis-persed to find cosy sleeping places, as wise pussies do after a com-fortable meal, we all thought that our little party had been brilliantly successful…

Three Little Kittens

Three little kittens lost their mittens,
And they began to cry:
'O, mother dear,
We sadly fear,
That we have lost our mittens!'

'Lost your mittens, you naughty kittens!
Then you shall have no pie!'
'Meeow, meeow, meeow!'
'No, you shall have no pie.'
'Meeow, meeow, meeow!'

The three little kittens found their mittens,
And they began to cry,
'O mother dear,
See here, see here!
See, we have found our mittens!'

'Put on your mittens, you silly kittens,
And you may have some pie.'
'O purr, purr, purr,
Oh, let us taste the pie!
Purr, purr, purr.'

The three little kittens put on their mittens,
And soon ate up the pie.
'Oh, mother dear,
We greatly fear,
That we have soiled our mittens!'

'Soiled your mittens! you naughty kittens.'
And they began to sigh:
'Meeow, meeow, meeow!'
Then they began to sigh:
'Meeow, meeow, meeow!'

The three little kittens washed their mittens
And hung them out to dry,
'Oh mother dear,
Do you not hear,
That we have washed our mittens?'

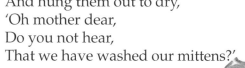

'Washed your mittens! Then
    you're good kittens:
But I smell a rat close by.'
'Hush, hush! Meeow, meeow!
We smell a rat close by!
Meeow, meeow, meeow.'

ANONYMOUS

[69]

Two Little Kittens

Two little kittens, one stormy night,
Began to quarrel and then to fight;
One had a mouse, the other had none,
And that was the way the quarrel begun.

'I'll have that mouse!' said the bigger cat;
'You'll have that mouse? We'll see about that.'
'I will have that mouse,' said the elder one;
'You shan't have that mouse,' said the little one.

I told you before 'twas a stormy night
When these two little kittens began to fight;
The old woman seized her sweeping broom
And swept the two kittens right out of the room.

The ground was covered with frost and snow,
And the two little kittens had nowhere to go:
So they laid them down on the mat at the door,
While the angry old woman was sweeping the floor.

And then they crept in as quiet as mice,
All wet with snow and as cold as ice,
For they found it was better that stormy night,
To lie down and sleep than to quarrel and fight.

ANONYMOUS

Two Final Nursery Rhymes

There was a little cat,
And she caught a little rat,
Which she dutifully rendered to her mother –
Who said, 'Bake him in a pie,
For his flavour's very high,
Or confer him on the poor, if you'd rather.'

MARK TWAIN

Pussy has a whiskered face,
Kitty has such pretty ways;
Doggie scampers when I call
And has a heart to love us all.

CHRISTINA ROSSETTI

If the most famous moment in nursery literature starts with a white rabbit (in *Alice In Wonderland*), then the second most famous beginning concerns kittens in *Alice Through the Looking Glass*.

One thing was certain, that the *white* kitten had had nothing to do with it: – it was the black kitten's fault entirely. For the white kitten had been having its face washed by the old cat for the last quarter of an hour (and bearing it pretty well, considering); so you see that it *couldn't* have had any hand in the mischief.

The way Dinah washed her children's faces was this: first she held the poor thing down by its ear with one paw, and then with the other paw she rubbed its face all over, the wrong way, beginning at the nose: and just now, as I said, she was hard at work on the white kitten, which was lying quite still and trying to purr – no doubt feeling that it was all meant for its own good.

But the black kitten had been finished with earlier in the afternoon, and so, while Alice was sitting curled up in a corner of the great armchair, half talking to herself and half asleep, the kitten had been having a grand game of romps with the ball of worsted Alice had been trying to wind up, and had been rolling it up and down till it had all come undone again; and there it was, spread over the hearthrug, all knots and tangles, with the kitten running after its own tail in the middle.

'Oh you wicked, wicked little thing!' cried Alice, catching up the kitten, and giving it a little kiss to make it understand that it was in disgrace. 'Really, Dinah ought to have taught you better manners! You *ought*, Dinah, you know you ought!' she added, looking reproachfully at the old cat, and speaking in as cross a voice as she could manage – and then she scrambled back into the armchair, taking the kitten and worsted with her, and began winding up the ball again. But she didn't get on very fast, as she was talking all the time, sometimes to the kitten, and sometimes to herself. Kitty sat very demurely on her knee, pretending to watch the progress of the winding, and now and then putting out one paw and gently touching the ball, as if it would be glad to help if it might...

Alice wound two or three turns of the worsted round the kitten's neck, just to see how it would look: this led to a scramble, in which the ball rolled down upon the floor, and yards and yards of it got unwound again...

'Let's pretend that you're the Red Queen, Kitty! Do you know, I think if you sat up and folded your arms you'd look exactly like her. Now do try, there's a dear!' And Alice got the Red Queen off the table, and set it up before the kitten as a model for it to imitate; however, the thing didn't succeed, principally, Alice said, because the kitten wouldn't fold its arms properly. So, to punish it, she held it up to the Looking glass, that it might see how sulky it was '– and if you're not good directly,' she added, 'I'll put you through into Looking-glass House. How would you like *that*?'

THE END OF KITTENHOOD

The end of kittenhood comes only too soon for many little ones. Kittens are left to starve in the farmyards at the onset of winter, abandoned by the side of a motorway, or simply thrown out into the streets to be run over. Tiny and vulnerable, as all young creatures are, only a few of the unwanted kittens have a chance of survival.

Even when a kitten is wanted and treasured, we lose it. The fearless little scrap of a playful kitten becomes a sleek, clever, subtle cat. 'For point of size she is likely to be a kitten always, being extremely small of her age, but time, I suppose, that spoils everything, will make her also a cat,' wrote the poet William Cowper gloomily of one of his favourites. 'No wisdom that she may gain by experience, and reflect hereafter, will compensate the loss of her present hilarity.'

Robert Southey, who compared kittens with rosebuds, also complained, 'The rose loses only something in delicacy by its development – enough to make it a serious emblem to a pensive mind; but if a cat could remember kittenhood, as we remember our youth, it were enough to break a cat's heart, even if it had nine times nine heart strings.'

Yet is this fair? It is one of the miracles of the common daily life that the kitten is not always dead – it can live on, with all its playfulness and innocence, in the graceful body of the adult cat. Anxious cats, unhappy cats or cats that are hunting all day just to survive, rarely exhibit this inner kittenhood.

Yet in moments of calm and happiness, and such moments occur for a cat in a safe and happy home, the full-grown cat will play like a kitten. Even more touchingly, the full-grown cat sometimes becomes a kitten on our laps. Its paws start kneading with the action of a tiny blind baby creature seeking the comfort of its mother's nipple. For there are times when its response to us is that of a kitten – trust, tenderness, simplicity and love.

These are the spiritual virtues of a human life – one reason perhaps why Florence Nightingale saw God in her cats. The writer Antonia White certainly thought fit to thank God for her kittens, when in her diary for 1954 she was summing up the year that was about to pass: 'Our Lady has showered me with kindness all the year … even to the two kittens.' Other writers have persuaded themselves that in that Bethlehem stable two thousand years ago there must have been a cat with kittens.

There is in the kittenhood of the adult cat something that we grown-up humans might well imitate. For the kitten in the cat can bring out the child that lives in every adult human being, and this child, so Christians would say, brings us into the kingdom of heaven. Happy the human and the cat that knows how to play. In the mischief and delight of kittens, we are close to the very heartbeat of the divine.

The American poet Ogden Nash has succinctly summed up the sadness of losing the kitten in the cat.

The Kitten

The trouble with a kitten is
THAT
Eventually it becomes a
CAT.

Joanna Baillie's poem, *The Kitten*, ends on a sombre note. She is conscious that when kittens grow into cats, they may no longer be loved and petted as once they were.

Whence hast thou then, thou witless puss!
The magic power to charm us thus?
Is it that in thy glaring eye
And rapid movements, we descry –
Whilst we at ease, secure from ill,
The chimney corner snugly fill –
A lion darting on his prey,
A tiger at his ruthless play?
Or is it that in thee we trace,
With all thy varied wanton grace,
An emblem, viewed with kindred eye,
Of tricky, restless infancy?
Ah! many a lightly sportive child,
Who hath like thee our wits beguiled,
To dull and sober manhood grown,
With strange recoil our hearts disown.

And so, poor kit! must thou endure,
When thou becom'st a cat demure,
Full many a cuff and angry word,
Chased roughly from the tempting board.
But yet, for that thou hast, I ween,
So oft our favoured playmate been,
Soft be the change which thou shalt prove!
When time hath spoiled thee of our love,
Still be thou deemed by housewife fat
A comely, careful, mousing cat,
Whose dish is, for the public good,
Replenished oft with savoury food,
Nor, when thy span of life is past,
Be thou to pond or dunghill cast,
But, gently borne on goodman's spade,
Beneath the decent sod be laid;
And children show with glistening eyes
The place where poor old pussy lies.

Essayist Jerome K. Jerome, with more sympathy than some, mourned the metamorphosis of kitten into cat. He saw in it not just the sadness of losing the kitten, but also our own sadness at losing our youth.

Ah me! Life sadly changes us all. Look even at Pussy Sobersides, with her dull sleepy glance, her grave slow walk, and dignified, prudish airs; who could ever think that once she was the blue-eyed, whirling, scampering, head-over-heels, mad little firework that we call a kitten.

What marvellous vitality a kitten has. It is really something very beautiful the way life bubbles over in the little creatures. They rush about, and mew, and spring; dance on their hind legs, embrace everything with their front ones, roll over and over and over, lie on their backs and kick. They don't know what to do with themselves, they are so full of life.

Can you remember, reader, when you and I felt something of the same sort of thing? Oh that magnificent young LIFE! that crowned us kings of the earth; that rushed through every tingling vein, till we seemed to walk on air; that thrilled through our throbbing brains, and told us to go forth and conquer the whole world; that welled up in our young hearts, till we longed to stretch out our arms and gather all the toiling men and women and the little children to our breast, and love them all – all. Ah, our pulse beats slow and steady now, and our old joints are rheumatic, and we love our easy chair and pipe, and sneer at boys' enthusiasm. But oh! for one brief moment of that god-like life again.

Charles Darwin, who changed the world's thinking with his theory of evolution, wrote a book entitled *The Expression of the Emotions in Man and Animals*. Here he comments on the kitten-like habit of cats kneading soft bedding.

Kittens, puppies, young pigs and probably many other young animals, alternately push with their fore-feet against the mammary glands of their mothers, to excite a freer secretion of milk, or to make it flow. Now it is very common with young cats, and not at all rare with old cats of the common and Persian breeds (believed by some naturalists to be specifically extinct), when comfortably lying on a warm shawl or other soft substance, to pound it quietly and alternately with their fore-feet; their toes being spread out and claws slightly protruded, precisely as when sucking their mother. That it is the same movement is clearly shown by their often at the same time taking a bit of the shawl into their mouths and sucking it; generally closing their eyes and purring from delight. This curious movement is commonly excited only in association with the sensation of a warm soft surface; but I have seen an old cat, when pleased by having its back scratched, pounding the air with its feet in the same manner; so that this action has almost become the expression of a pleasurable sensation.

Gideon Ousley, a somewhat eccentric cat lover, wrote an apocryphal gospel called *The Gospel of the Holy Twelve,* although in his introduction, he claimed that his work was a fragment of an early gospel preserved in a Buddhist monastery in Tibet. Gideon Ousley felt that 'when our Saviour brought redemption to a world sunk in selfishness, hard-heartedness and misery and proclaimed the Gospel of an all-embracing love, there was surely a share in this redemption for all suffering creatures.' He went rather too far, though, in making up the evidence to prove it. Here is his version of the nativity.

And Joseph with Mary also went up from Galilee, out of the city of Nazareth into Judaea, unto the city of David, which is called Bethlehem (because they were of the house and lineage of David), to be taxed with Mary his espoused wife, who was great with child.

And so it was, that while they were there, the days were accomplished that she should be delivered. And she brought forth her firstborn child in a Cave, and wrapped him in swaddling clothes, and laid him in a manger, which was in the cave; because there was no room for them in the inn. And behold it was filled with many lights, bright as the Sun in his glory.

And there were in the same cave an ox, and a horse, and an ass and a sheep, and beneath the manger was a cat with her little ones...

A Kitten in Church

I have only once seen a pussy in church. It was not a parish church, but the chapel of one of the great London hospitals. The congregation was assembled and was awaiting the entrance of the chaplain, when a young pussy of an age somewhere between cat and kitten solemnly marched with tail erect, up the middle gangway. Without hesitation, and as if fulfilling a usual duty, he made for the reading desk, entered it, and for an instant was lost to view. But a moment later head and shoulder appeared above the desk, and a small wise face looked round with an air of quiet assurance and professional unconcern. I quite expected to see the little paws reverently folded, and to hear a tiny voice say: 'Let us purr'!

GERTRUDE JEKYLL

Sir Edward Dennison Ross was a professor of Persian and a lover of cats. He only wrote one poem, *A Traffic Martyr*. It is an elegy to a kitten that strayed into St James's Court and was adopted by the residents there. It isn't a great poem but its simplicity makes it touching.

His coat was partly black as ink,
And partly white as snow
When it was clean, and that is why
We called him 'Domino'.

He came from nowhere suddenly,
And claimed us all as friends,
And as he wasn't anyone's
He lived on odds and ends.

But little Domino is dead,
A big wheel squashed him flat,
And with him died the sweetest thing
That only was a cat.

He's gone where all the kittens go
That are too good for earth,
The Paradise of little cats
And puppies drowned at birth.

On Maou Dying at the Age of Six Months

Strange sickness fell upon this perfect creature
Who walked the equal friend of Man and Nature.
Her little Bodie, e'en as by a shroud,
Lay lapped in its unseen, dishevelling cloud;
Till to her eyes, unasking but afraid,
The old reply of endless night was made.

FRANCES CORNFORD

This poem, entitled *Minoushka*, was not written as an epitaph. Alas, it became one. Three hours after Gerard Benson had finished it, Minoushka demanded to go out and was never seen again. 'Two days later, a neighbour found her body stretched out looking as if she was sleep under a bush in the front garden. We buried her. I had no spirit for redrafting the poem.' It seems right, therefore, to use at the end of this book a poem recalling the happiness of an individual kitten.

The leaves swirl in the wind,
Yellow and gold and brown;
And, brown and gold, Minou
Hunts them up and down,
A tiny frisking clown.

A whisking, frisking scrap,
She bends in the afternoon sun.
She tumbles after her leaf,
Choosing a particular one:
Pounce! and the game is done.

Then she slinks, a minute panther,
The leaf gripped in her jaws,
Across the October grass,
To fetch her trophy indoors
Padding on delicate paws.

Resting beside the fire
Or on a convenient knee,
Minoushka stretches and yawns,
And (shame that such truths must be)
Scuffs out a troublesome flea.

She fears no living creature;
Even with the terrier, Jack,
She dares to stand her ground
And camel her small back
All ready to attack.

Yet she is utterly loving,
Purring, soft and small,
Perfectly, it seems, domestic,
Ambushing me in the hall
Or tail-up by her bowl.

This loved one, whom we rescued
From the traffic of a busy street,
Rewards us with ease and mischief,
Usurps the choicest seat,
Wildly assaults our feet.

Acknowledgements

The authors wish to thank Nicholas Howard for his valuable help in compiling this anthology.

For permission to reproduce copyright material in this book, the authors and publisher gratefully acknowledge the following:

Gerard Benson, 16 Ashwell Rd, Manningham, Bradford 8, for permission to print 'Minoushka'; Constable Publishers and Penguin Books USA for an extract from *Antonia White: Diaries 1926–57* by Susan Chitty, editor. Copyright © 1991 by Susan Chitty. Used by permission of Viking Penguin, a division of Penguin Books USA Inc.; William Donald, DSC, Troutlets, Church St, Keswick, Cumbria, for the account of naval kittens; the Estate of Frances Cornford and Random House UK Ltd for 'On Maou Dying at the Age of Six Months' from *On a Calm Shore* by Frances Cornford, published by Hutchinson; James MacGibbon and New Directions, New York for 'Our Office Cat' from *Collected Poems of Stevie Smith*. Copyright © 1972 by Stevie Smith. Reprinted by permission of New Directions Publishing Corp.; Celia Haddon for the translation of Edmund Rostand's *'Le Petit Chat'* and Hippolyte Taine's *'L'Enfance'*; Little, Brown and Company and Curtis Brown Ltd, New York, for ' The Kitten' from *Verses From 1929 On* and *The Face is Familiar* by Ogden Nash. Copyright © 1940 by Ogden Nash. By permission of Little, Brown and Company and Curtis Brown Ltd; Routledge for an extract from *The Prose of John Clare*, edited by J. W. and Anne Tibble, published by Routledge & Kegan Paul, 1951; Times Newspapers Ltd for two articles from *The Times*, 7 September 1950 and 20 September 1950. Copyright © Times Newspapers Ltd 1950; Andrea Whittaker for the translation of Theodor Storm's *'Von Katzen'*.

Picture Credits

Miss Ann White's Kitten by George Stubbs, reproduced by courtesy of Roy Miles Gallery, Bruton Street, London, Wl; *Kittens in a Basket* by Brunille, by courtesy of Fine Art Photographic Library, London; *A Cat with Three Kittens* by Henriette Ronner-Knip, by courtesy of Fine Art Photographic Library, London; *The Favourite* by Wilhelm Schutze, by courtesy of Fine Art Photographic Library, London/Haynes Fine Art, Broadway; *The Artist's Assistant* by Marie Sophie Goerlich, by courtesy of Fine Art Photographic Library, London/Galerie George; *Mischief with the Hatbox* by Henriette Ronner-Knip, by courtesy of Fine Art Photographic Library, London.